DATE DUE

Reverence for Life

REVERENCE FOR
Life

The Words of Albert Schweitzer

Compiled by Harold E. Robles
Foreword by Rhena Schweitzer Miller

HarperSanFrancisco
A Division of HarperCollinsPublishers

REVERENCE FOR LIFE: *The Words of Albert Schweitzer*.
Collection copyright © 1993 by Harold Robles. Foreword
copyright © 1993 by Rhena Schweitzer Miller. All rights
reserved. Printed in the United States of America. No part
of this book may be used or reproduced in any manner
whatsoever without written permission except in the case
of brief quotations embodied in critical articles and reviews.
For information address HarperCollins Publishers, 10 East
53rd Street, New York, NY 10022.

FIRST EDITION

Library of Congress Cataloging-in-Publication Data
Schweitzer, Albert, 1875-1965.
    Reverence for life : the words of Albert Schweitzer /
    compiled by Harold E. Robles ; foreword by Rhena
    Schweitzer Miller. —1st ed.
        p. cm.
    Includes bibliographical references and index.
    ISBN 0-06-067098-3 (hard : alk. paper)
    1. Life. 2. Peace. I. Robles, Harold E.
B2430.S373R48 1993
193—dc20   92-56137
                                                    CIP

93 94 95 96 97 HAD 10 9 8 7 6 5 4 3 2 1
This edition is printed on acid-free paper that meets the
American National Standards Institute Z39.48 Standard.

To Phoebe Berman,
with sincere respect
and devotion

Epigraph

In recent years I have been privileged to
see that my philosophy means something
to the world. My ethics of Reverence for Life
is beginning to come into its own, not only in
Europe but in the whole world. The ideal of
power is replaced by the ideal of kindness, not
only toward people but also toward every living
thing. This idea of kindness toward humans
and all creatures is now recognized as part of
true civilization. This is a success I would
not have dared to hope for.

—Albert Schweitzer,
in a letter to an old friend, 1964

Contents

Foreword

Already at an early age, my father, Albert Schweitzer, decided to make his life his argument. After intensive studies and major contributions in philosophy, theology, and music, he felt impelled to follow Jesus, whom he called his Master, by becoming a physician and surgeon so that he could provide medical care for the suffering people around Lambaréné, in the equatorial African forest.

It was in Africa that he found the concept of Reverence for Life, which became the basis for his thought and action and eventually, in his eighties, led him to speak out courageously and forcefully against the danger of nuclear arms.

For my father, Reverence for Life demands of each of us greater responsibility toward all that lives. He felt that not only does it unite us with all life on our planet, but that it affords us a spiritual relationship with the Universe.

Although living for half a century far from the great centers of the world, my father's voice from Lambaréné was heard when he spoke out his beliefs. That he had given these beliefs concrete realization in the form of his village hospital added to his credibility. The world he created in the African forest on the basis of Reverence for Life was a place where people of all colors, creeds, and nationalities could live together in harmony with each other and with the wild and domestic animals, where trees and plants were respected, and where life was taken only when it was a necessity.

Albert Schweitzer has been the guiding light of Harold Robles's life since he was eight years old, and this has compelled him to communicate to those around him in ever-widening circles the meaning and the importance of my father's philosophy.

In this book, *Reverence for Life: The Words of Albert Schweitzer*, Harold Robles has compiled quotations of my father according to the seven divisions of the Albert Schweitzer Institute for the Humanities, of which he is the founder and president. Although it was not always easy to assign these words to exact categories, you will find here the words of Schweitzer the philosopher, the man who followed Jesus, his Master; the words of the musician for whom Bach was the great source of consolation; and the words of the man who saw in Reverence for Life the basis for a more viable and ethical civilization.

Among these well-chosen quotations, I believe everyone can find more than a few words that are meaningful to him or her, words that will help all of us to become more sensitive and thoughtful human beings, who can thereby learn to live in greater harmony with the people and other living beings with whom we share this planet.

—Rhena Schweitzer Miller

Acknowledgments

I am deeply grateful to Hilary Vartanian of Harper San Francisco for her great interest in this project and in the activities of the Albert Schweitzer Institute, and to James Pouilliard and David Miller.

I also wish to extend my heartfelt thanks to Rhena Schweitzer Miller and my wife, Ruth D'Agostino, for their helpful input and continuing loving support.

Introduction

"In the summer of 1915, I took my wife, who was in poor health, to Port-Gentil on the Atlantic. I brought the meager drafts of my proposed book the *Philosophy of Civilization* along. In September, I received word that the wife of the Swiss missionary, Pelot, had fallen ill at their mission in N'Gomo, and that I was expected to make a medical call there. The mission was 120 miles upstream on the Ogowe River. My only means of immediate transportation was a small old steamboat. We advanced slowly on our trip upstream. It was the dry season, and we had to feel our way through huge sandbanks. Before boarding the steamer, I had resolved to devote the entire trip to the problem of how a culture could be brought into being, that possessed a greater moral depth and energy than the one we lived in. I filled page after page with disconnected sentences, primarily to center my every thought on the problem. At sunset of the third day, near the village of Igendja, we moved along an island set in the middle of the wide river. On a sandbank to our left, four hippopotami and their young plodded along in our direction. Just then, in my great tiredness and discouragement, there flashed upon my mind, unforeseen and unsought, the phrase, 'Reverence for Life.' The iron door had yielded: the path in the thicket had become visible. Now I had found my way to the idea in which affirmation of the world and ethics are contained side by side! As far as I knew, it was a phrase I had never heard nor ever read. I realized at once that it carried within itself the solution to the problem that had been torturing me. Only by means of reverence for life can we establish a spiritual and humane relationship with both people and all living creatures within our reach."

Rarely has any man excelled in so many branches of learning and spent his days in such unselfish service. Eminent as a philosopher, theologian, musician, and physician, Albert Schweitzer considered the relief of suffering the main purpose of his life, and the hospital he founded and maintained for so many years on the edge of an African forest will be his chief memorial. People may not accept his reasoning, may disagree with his criticism, or may challenge his exposition of Bach, but everyone can appreciate his desire to serve humanity.

Albert Schweitzer was born on January 14, 1875, at Kaysersberg, Upper Alsace, where his father was pastor and his mother a minister's daughter. He was six months old when his father was transferred to Gunsbach in the Münster Valley, where Albert grew up with an older sister, two younger sisters, and a younger brother. The church at Gunsbach fascinated Albert Schweitzer from early boyhood. Having begun to study the piano when he was five and the organ when he was eight, he was permitted by the age of nine to substitute for the organist at church services. After a year in the gymnasium at Münster, Albert Schweitzer went to the high school in Mulhausen, and from there he entered Strasbourg University. He studied the organ under Eugene Munch, finding particular enjoyment in improvisation. At Strasbourg University he studied philosophy and theology and in 1898 gained a scholarship that took him to Paris and Berlin. A year later he received his first degree, a Ph.D., for a thesis on Kant's Philosophy of Religion (*Die Religionsphilosophie Kants*).

While in Paris, Albert Schweitzer took organ lessons from Charles Marie Widor and piano lessons from Marie Jael-Trautmann. At the suggestion of Widor he wrote a biography of Johann Sebastian Bach, which was published in French (*Jean Sebastien Bach*) in 1905 and then completely rewritten for a German edition (*Johann Sebastian Bach*), published in 1908. Both his biography of Bach and his critical editing of Bach's organ works are considered authoritative. All this time he continued his duties at Strasbourg, ministering to his congregation and later becoming the principal of the Theological College of St. Thomas.

In 1906 came his epoch-making work, *Von Reimarus zu Wrede: Eine Geschichte der Leben-Jesu-Forschung,* published in English as *The Quest of the Historical Jesus.* In this and other theological works Schweitzer stressed the eschatological views (concerned with the idea of the last days of history) perceived in the lives of Jesus and the apostle Paul. He shattered skeptical attempts to disprove the historical existence of Jesus. The argument of *The Quest of the Historical Jesus* gained Schweitzer great prominence in the ranks of New Testament scholars, for it rehabilitated the historical significance of Matthew's Gospel by proving that Jesus's involvement in late Jewish eschatology completely and firmly rooted him in that period and showed for believers that Jesus's claims to authority demand not merely recognition but obedience.

In Strasbourg, Schweitzer was occupied with charitable work among the city's homeless people and released prisoners, but these humanitarian efforts did not satisfy him. As his later autobiographical books reveal, suffering to him was the great mystery. Even as a schoolboy he often wondered why he should be happy and others suffer.

A turning point in his career came in the autumn of 1904 when he happened to read an article on the needs of the Congo Mission in a magazine published by the Paris Missionary Society. He determined to devote himself until he was thirty to science and art but, from that time on, to give himself to the direct service of humanity. Albert Schweitzer thus spent the next seven years, from 1905 to 1912, in the study of medicine, obtaining his M.D. degree in 1913.

During his medical training, he remained on the faculty of the University of Strasbourg and continued to give organ concerts to earn money for his projected mission, which he also financed through royalties from his books on Jesus and Bach. For his medical thesis he wrote a psychiatric study of Jesus, *Die Psychiatrische*

Beurteilung Jesu (The Psychiatric Study of Jesus), refuting the theory that Jesus suffered from paranoia. Although a theologian, Schweitzer had decided to go to Africa as a medical missionary rather than a preacher. As he explained later in his book *Aus Meiner Kindheit und Jugendzeit (Memoirs of Childhood and Youth),* "This new form of activity I could not represent to myself as being talking about the religion of love, but only as an actual putting it into practice."

On Good Friday, 1913, he left for French Equatorial Africa accompanied by his wife, Helene Bresslau, whom he had married in 1912. She had already trained as a nurse. Their destination was Lambaréné in Gabon, eight hundred miles up the river Ogowe, where the Paris Missionary Society gave him land on which to build a hospital at his expense. Sixteen months after the Schweitzers' arrival in Africa, when World War I broke out, they were interned as enemy aliens. They were later allowed to work at the hospital but in the fall of 1917 were sent to France as prisoners of war. There they were held in internment camps until their release in July 1918.

Albert Schweitzer's seven-year absence from Lambaréné gave him an opportunity to think and write that would have been impossible at his jungle hospital. He spent the first years in Strasbourg, as preacher at St. Nicholas and as a doctor at the City Hospital. He also gave organ concerts in Barcelona and other cities of Europe, as well as lectures in Sweden, England, and other countries. On his forty-fourth birthday in 1919, Mrs. Schweitzer presented her husband with her most unique birthday gift, a baby girl named Rhena. During this time, Schweitzer devoted most of his attention to philosophy and religion, completing the first two volumes of his projected four-volume *The Philosophy of Civilization*. The two volumes, *The Decay and Restoration of Civilization* and *Civilization and Ethics,* were published in German in 1923 and in English in 1929 and 1932. In analyzing contemporary civilization, Schweitzer found that "the abdication of thought has been the decisive factor in the collapse of civilization." In his second volume he discussed his ideas on the reconstruction of civilization, including "Reverence for Life," his ethical principle involving all living things, which he believed essential to the survival of civilization.

It was 1924 before Schweitzer got back to Lambaréné, this time without his wife, whose health prevented her accompanying him. He found his hospital in ruins, but this gave him the opportunity to erect better buildings on a site with more space higher up the river. The new hospital was inaugurated in 1927 and continually expanded until his death in 1965.

His task was financially eased by his fame, which was spread by his autobiographical and other writings and by eyewitness reports from visitors and reporters to Lambaréné. His example of dedication brought many men and women, often medically trained, to the hospital in Lambaréné for varying periods of service. International honors—including many doctorates from universities throughout the world, the Goethe Prize of Frankfurt (1928), the Nobel Peace Prize (1952), the Order of Merit (1955), the German Order Pour le Merite

(1955), the Sonning Prize (1959)—also made his hospital a global point of interest. He continued to work without a holiday.

In 1949, Schweitzer, then 74, made his one and only visit to the United States to address the Goethe bicentenary festival at Aspen, Colorado. To his surprise, Aspen turned out to be 8,000 feet high, a great deal higher than anything in the Vosges of France, and the altitude did not suit him. "Aspen," he said, "is built too close to heaven." His first lecture, in French, was translated by Dr. Emory Ross, and his second, in German, by the novelist and playwright Thornton Wilder. Those who knew him said that he lived by Goethe's principle, "Do good for the pure love of Good." On their way back to New York, the Schweitzers visited Chicago, Cleveland, and Boston. The University of Chicago presented him with the honorary degree of Doctor of Laws.

The seal of international approval was set on Albert Schweitzer's life and work by the honors bestowed on him in his last years. He was awarded the Nobel Peace Prize for 1952 and went to Oslo in 1954 to receive the gold medal and the diploma of the award. His Nobel Peace Prize address, "Das Problem des Friedens in der heutigen Welt" ("The Problem of Peace in the World Today"), had a worldwide circulation. It was characteristic of Schweitzer that he used the Nobel monetary prize to help build a special village for his leprosy patients in Lambaréné. In 1955 Queen Elizabeth conferred upon him Great Britain's highest civilian award, the Order of Merit.

In 1957 Mrs. Schweitzer passed away in Switzerland, having just returned from her final visit to her husband in Lambaréné. Her long years of toil and dedication at her husband's side were over.

In 1958 Dr. Schweitzer went on record as opposing further atomic weapons tests because of the danger of radioactive fallout. He urged the superpowers, in the name of humanity, to renounce nuclear testing. He corresponded with President Eisenhower and with other world leaders in an effort to end such testing. It became the beginning of the change of public opinion that led to the limited nuclear test ban in the last year of the Kennedy administration.

The remaining years of Albert Schweitzer's life were spent in the quiet jungle along the Ogowe River administering to the people of Gabon. Despite increasing criticisms of his medical practice as autocratic and primitive, and despite the opposition sometimes raised against his theological works, Albert Schweitzer's influence continues to have a strong and unique moral appeal, serving as a source of encouragement to many. By his example and devoted service to suffering humanity, Dr. Schweitzer tested the conscience of all people. And he gave to the world a philosophy, one by which he lived his life and which he felt expressed the hope and promise of civilization. He called it "Ehrfurcht vor den Leben," Reverence for Life.

Harold E. Robles

Reverence for Life

I   THE MARK OF PAIN

Health and Well-Being

Those to whom good things happen in their lives must feel called upon to give of their lives in order to alleviate misery.

I could not but feel with a sympathy full of regret all the pain that I saw around me, not only that of men, but that of the whole creation. From this community of suffering, I have never tried to withdraw myself. It seemed to me a matter of course that we should all take our share of the burden of pain which lies upon the world.

On the Edge of the Primeval Forest, 1921

The fellowship of those who bear the mark of pain. Who are the members of this fellowship? Those who have learned by experience what physical pain and bodily anguish mean belong together all over the world; they are united by a secret bond. One and all they know the horrors of suffering to which man can be exposed, and one and all they know the longing to be free from pain. He who has been delivered from pain must not think he is now free again and at liberty to take life up just as it was before, entirely forgetful of the past. He is now a "man whose eyes are open" with regard to pain and anguish, and he must help to overcome those two enemies and to bring to others the deliverance which he has himself enjoyed.

On the Edge of the Primeval Forest, 1921

Whoever among us has through personal experience learned what pain and anxiety really are must help to ensure that those who out there are in bodily need obtain the help which came to him. He belongs no more to himself alone; he has become the brother of all who suffer. On the "brotherhood of those who bear the mark of pain" lies the duty of medical work, work for humanity's sake.

Out of My Life and Thought, 1931

I have not lost courage. The misery I have seen gives me strength, and faith in my fellow men supports my confidence in the future. I do hope that I shall find a sufficient number of people who, because they themselves have been saved from physical suffering, will respond to requests on behalf of those who are in similar need. . . . I do hope that among the doctors of the world there will soon be several besides myself who will be sent out, here and there in the world, by "the fellowship of those who bear the mark of pain."

On the Edge of the Primeval Forest, 1921

Pain is the more terrible lord of mankind than even death itself.

On the Edge of the Primeval Forest, 1921

I wanted to be a doctor that I might be able to work without having to talk. For years I have been giving myself out in words. . . . This new form of activity I could not represent to myself as talking about the religion of love, but only as an actual putting it into practice.

Memoirs of Childhood and Youth, 1924

The mother who owes it to medical aid that her child still belongs to her, and not to the cold earth, must help, so that the poor mother who has never seen a doctor may be spared what she has been spared.

On the Edge of the Primeval Forest, 1921

Whoever is spared personal pain must feel himself called upon to help in diminishing the pain of others. We must all carry our share of the misery which lies upon the world.

Memoirs of Childhood and Youth, 1924

The deeper piety is, the humbler are its claims with regard to knowledge of the suprasensible. It is like a path which winds between the hills instead of going over them.

Out of My Life and Thought, 1931

ॐ

There are no heroes of action, only heroes of renunciation and suffering.

Out of My Life and Thought, 1931

ॐ

You have never experienced pain and suffering like others to whom a sickbed has become a trusted place and who can little more think of a life in normal health than others can of paradise.

"What Does It Mean to Be a Person to Another Person?"
sermon preached on June 15, 1919

How can death be overcome? By regarding, in moments of deepest concentration, our lives and those who are part of our lives as though we already had lost them in death, only to receive them back for a little while.

"Overcoming Death," sermon preached on November 17, 1907

If mankind is not to perish after all the dreadful things it has done and gone through, then a new spirit must emerge. And this new spirit is coming not with a roar but with a quiet birth, not with grand measures and words but with an imperceptible change in the atmosphere—a change in which each of us is participating and which each of us regards as a quiet boon.

Letter to a youth leader in Germany, 1959

It is unthinkable that we civilized peoples should keep for ourselves alone the wealth of means for fighting sickness, pain, and death which science has given us. If there is any ethical thinking at all among us, how can we refuse to let new discoveries benefit those who, in distant lands, are subject to even greater physical distress than we are?

Out of My Life and Thought, 1931

On the "brotherhood of those who bear the mark of pain" lies the duty of medical work, work for humanity's sake, in the colonies. Commissioned by their representatives, medical men must accomplish among the suffering in far-off lands what is crying out for accomplishment in the name of true civilization. In reliance upon the elementary truth which is embodied in the idea of the "brotherhood of those who bear the mark of pain," I ventured to found the Forest Hospital at Lambaréné.

Out of My Life and Thought, 1931

Where a man's death agony might have been terrible but could fortunately be made tolerable by a doctor's skill, those who stood around his deathbed must help, that others too may enjoy that same consolation when they lose their dear ones. Such is the fellowship of those who bear the mark of pain.

On the Edge of the Primeval Forest, 1921

❧

The idealism that I preach is no nebulous thing; it has stood the test of practical achievement. I am confident that a group of men who appeal without too much fanfare to the generosity of any country for the creation of a medical station in the midst of the most underprivileged colonial peoples will be listened to and will succeed in their plans, especially if they are resolved, contrary to present tendencies, to begin modestly.

"Medical Aid in the Colonies," article, 1931

❧

Again and again we unite with gratitude to the God who has directed us to such a glorious sphere of activity, gratitude to the kind people who make it possible for us through the gifts they send for the work.

"Busy Days in Lambaréné," article, 1934

I welcome the news that the large meeting of Japanese physicians will be dealing with the creation of the spirit of humanity and the role played by physicians in this undertaking. How I wish I could attend the discussions. Unfortunately, I cannot leave Lambaréné at this time. It is my deep conviction that we doctors who strive to preserve life are called upon in a special way to educate mankind to have reverence for life and thereby achieve a higher spiritual and ethical stance, which will enable people to grasp and solve the difficult problems of our era.

Letter to the Congress of Japanese Physicians, 1959

As pastor and doctor I have been able to gain insight into the great problem faced by those who have been denied the light of the eye or who have lost it. I have been moved by the way in which many of these persons have succeeded in triumphing over this fate. I have met blind persons who, through the peace that emanated from them, have become a blessing to those around them and to those they encountered. The struggle to cope with this condition is an especially difficult one for the war blind in every nation. We who have suffered no such hardships, or only minor ones, must sometimes feel embarrassed because we are so much better off, and we must bring to them more than the ordinary compassion. Those who have had to endure what we have been spared have a right to have us treat them with a constant understanding and kindly readiness to help.

Article for the Yearbook for the German War Blind, 1957

As a physician I can say that I know of people in despair who, for reasons of health, or when their mind is ill, desire to end their lives. We should not judge this as right or wrong. But sometimes people kill themselves because they have found no one to help them. They have lost hope in mankind. They have found no compassion. When we are truly filled with the idea of Reverence for Life, all our attitudes, thinking, actions change. We must go deep into ourselves to find inspiration. Slogans, publicity, and means of communication don't help us to find this philosophy. Nor is there one formula for everyone. But if we turn within, pondering our duty in this world in silence, and act to move toward this goal, a change will come about. There are many opportunities to prove that we live in the spirit of the philosophy of Reverence for Life.

In response to a question about suicide, interview in Copenhagen, 1959

I regard it as an advantage that I could establish this hospital during the period of the great struggle against sleeping sickness. The project has grown far beyond my expectations. It evolved because of donations from my friends and because of the doctors and nurses who came to help me. The capable Dutch nurses have played a major role in the history of the hospital because of the work they have accomplished and the spirit they have developed here. I owe Holland a great debt of thanks.

Letter to Queen Juliana of the Netherlands, April 26, 1963

Today mankind is living in a state of inhumanity, into which it has sunk because of wrong thinking and thoughtlessness and also because of the two horribly inhumane wars that were fought with horribly inhumane weapons. We must all jointly experience the yearning to become humane humans again.

Letter to Rabbi David Jacobson, 1962

I often think about Your Highness when the diesel motor hums and illuminates the operating room, which has been provided with the most modern furniture and equipment thanks to your generosity. For more than a year now I have been in Lambaréné, absorbed in making my hospital run as smoothly as possible, and I haven't had a day of rest, not even a real Sunday.

Letter to Prince Rainier III of Monaco, 1957

My warmest thanks for the Korean translation of my three speeches, *Peace or Atomic War?* You have given me great pleasure. I am trying to get these speeches circulated as widely as possible because I want to advance the argument that atomic weapons are contrary to international law. International law admits only weapons that have a limitable, local effect—that is, only those that destroy or injure the combatants they are aimed at, but not distant nonparticipants. I have developed this idea in these three speeches, and I hope that they are understood and that they help us to persuade the countries that own nuclear weapons to renounce them.

Letter to the Reverend Dr. Timothy Yilsun Rhee, 1958

2 THE FRIEND OF NATURE

Ecology and the Environment

We are not capable of resolving the mystery of the inhumanity ruling natural events. We can only find solace in the knowledge that we are called upon to be compassionate and want to be found true in this endeavor.

In the hope of reaching the moon men fail to see the flowers that blossom at their feet.

In conversation with the governor of Gabon, 1958

ॐ

What we seem to forget is that, yes, the sun will continue to rise and set and the moon will continue to move across the skies, but mankind can create a situation in which the sun and moon can look down upon an earth that has been stripped of all life.

"A Declaration of Conscience," speech, 1957

ॐ

In everything you recognize yourself. The tiny beetle that lies dead in your path—it was a living creature, struggling for existence like yourself, rejoicing in the sun like you, knowing fear and pain like you. And now it is no more than decaying matter—which is what you will be sooner or later too.

"Reverence for Life," sermon preached on February 16, 1919

฿

I am aware of some of the tragic repercussions of the chemical fight against insects taking place in France and elsewhere, and I deplore them. Modern man no longer knows how to foresee or to forestall. He will end by destroying the earth from which he and other living creatures draw their food. Poor bees, poor birds, poor men . . .

Letter to French beekeeper, 1956

฿

The God of love who meets us in love cannot be united with the God who encounters us in nature. The ethical law cannot be made consonant with the laws of nature.

"Conduct Toward Life Around Us: Animals, Plants,"
sermon preached on March 2, 1919

&

The traveler on the plain sees from afar the distant range of mountains. Then he loses sight of them again. His way winds slowly upwards through the valleys, drawing ever nearer to the peaks, until at last, at a turn of the path, they stand before him, not in the shapes which they had seemed to take from the distant plain, but in their actual forms.

The Quest of the Historical Jesus, 1926

&

The deeper we look into nature, the more we realize that it is full of life, and the more profoundly we know that all life is a secret and that we are united with all life that is in nature. Man can no longer live for himself alone. We must realize that all life is valuable and that we are united to all life. From this knowledge comes our spiritual relationship to the Universe.

"Busy Days in Lambaréné," article, 1934

The friend of nature is the man who feels himself inwardly united with everything that lives in nature, who shares in the fate of all creatures, helps them when he can in their pain and need, and as far as possible avoids injuring or taking life.

"The Revival of Falconry," article, 1932

It seems almost something abnormal that over a portion of the earth's surface nature should be nothing and man everything.

More from the Primeval Forest, 1931

River and forest . . . ! Who can really describe the first impression they make? We seemed to be dreaming! Pictures of antediluvian scenery which elsewhere had seemed to be merely the creation of fancy, are now seen in real life. It is impossible to say where the river ends and the lands begins, for a mighty network of roots, clothed with bright flowering creepers, projects right into the water.

On the Edge of the Primeval Forest, 1921

How much effort it will take for us to get men to understand the words of Jesus, "Blessed are the merciful," and to bring them to realization that their responsibility includes all creatures. But we must struggle with courage.

Letter to James Sinclair, 1959

❧

A man is really ethical only when he obeys the constraint laid on him to aid all life which he is able to help, and when he goes out of his way to avoid injuring anything living. He does not ask how far this or that life deserves sympathy as valuable in itself, nor how far it is capable of feeling. To him life as such is sacred.

Philosophy of Civilization, Part 2, 1923

❧

We are born of other lives. . . . We possess the capacities to bring still other lives into existence. So nature compels us to recognize the fact of mutual dependence, each life necessarily helping the other lives which are linked to it.

"The Ethics of Reverence for Life," article, 1936

It hurts me to think that we never acknowledge the absolutely mysterious character of Nature, but always speak so confidently of explaining her, whereas all that we have really done is to go into full and more complicated descriptions which only make the mysterious more mysterious than ever.

Memoirs of Childhood and Youth, 1924

Profound love demands a deep conception and out of this develops reverence for the mystery of life. It brings us close to all beings. To the poorest and smallest, as well as all others. We reject the idea that man is "master of other creatures," "lord" above all others. We bow to reality. We no longer say that there are senseless existences with which we can deal as we please. We recognize that all existence is a mystery, like our own existence. The poor fly which we would like to kill with our hands has come into existence like ourselves. It knows anxiety, it knows hope for happiness, it knows fear of not existing any more. Has any man so far been able to create a fly? That is why our neighbor is not only man: my neighbor is a creature like myself, subject to the same joys, the same fears, and the idea of Reverence for Life gives us something more profound and mightier than the idea of humanism. It includes *all living beings.*

From notes, Brussels, 1959

As long as I can remember, I have suffered because of the great misery I saw in the world. I never really knew the artless, youthful joy of living, and I believe that many children feel this way, even when outwardly they seem to be wholly happy and without a single care. I used to suffer particularly because the poor animals must endure so much pain and want. The sight of an old, limping horse being dragged along by one man while another man struck him with a stick—he was being driven to the slaughterhouse—tortured me for weeks.

Memoirs of Childhood and Youth, 1924

I cannot but have reverence for all that is called life. I cannot avoid compassion for everything that is called life. That is the beginning and foundation of morality.

"Reverence for Life," sermon preached on February 16, 1919

❧

Even when I was a child I was like a person in an ecstasy in the presence of Nature, without anyone suspecting it. I consider Nature as the great consoler. In her I always found calm and serenity again when I was disturbed. And this has only become accentuated during the course of my life.

Letter to American poet Hermann Hagedorn, December 16, 1944

❧

Nature looks beautiful and marvelous when you view it from the outside. But when you read its pages like a book, it is horrible.

"Ethics of Compassion," sermon preached on February 23, 1919

꘎

The soul is the sense of something higher than ourselves, something that stirs in us thoughts, hopes, and aspirations which go out to the world of goodness, truth, and beauty.

"My Brother's Keeper," sermon preached on April 4, 1909

꘎

When necessity leads us, we arrogate to ourselves the right to wreak massive destruction, and we can do no other. But precisely because we do stand so clearly under the terrible law of nature, which permits living beings to kill other living beings, we must watch with anxiety that we do not destroy out of thoughtlessness.

"Conduct Toward Life Around Us: Animals, Plants,"
sermon preached on March 2, 1919

❧

Our true relationship to living creatures has not become obvious to us, because that general principle belongs there—Reverence for Life as such, the great sharing—as the great understanding of life. Everything else remains imperfect and is built on sand.

"Conduct Toward Life Around Us: Animals, Plants,"
sermon preached on March 2, 1919

❧

The fact that in nature one creature may cause pain to another and even deal with it instinctively in the most cruel way, is a harsh mystery that weighs upon us as long as we live. One who has reached the point where he does not suffer ever and again because of this has really ceased to be a man.

"The Revival of Falconry," article, March 1932

3 LOVE WIDENED INTO UNIVERSALITY

Theology and Philosophy

The idea that true piety consists in being in the world but not of the world retains its truth for all times.

He comes to us as One unknown, without a name, as of old, by the lakeside, He came to those men who knew Him not. He speaks to us the same word, "Follow thou me," and sets us to the tasks which He has to fulfill for our time. He commands. And to those who obey Him, whether they be wise or simple, He will reveal Himself in the toils, the conflicts, the sufferings which they shall pass through in His fellowship, and, as an ineffable mystery, they shall learn in their own experience Who HE is.

The Quest of the Historical Jesus, 1906

The world expects highly effective ideas. It demands a labor that is performed in the spirit of the Gospel and that is also in proper order and achieves its goal. It expects the spirit to transform the given reality. What you owe the world is this: to move all goodwill to an enthusiastic, personal, and sensible commitment. Therein lies the great problem. Whatever you do toward this end will arouse people of goodwill throughout the world and encourage them to lend a hand in other countries. May God grant you wisdom and strength to make the Gospel shine in the darkness of this world.

Letter to Abbé Pierre, 1954

I decided that I would make my life my argument. I would advocate the things I believed in, in terms of the life I lived and what I did.

Letter to Norman Cousins, 1958

❧

It was unreasonable to me—this was even before I had gone to school—that in my evening devotions I should pray only for people. So when my mother had prayed with me and kissed me goodnight, I used secretly to add another prayer which I had myself composed for all living creatures. It ran like this: "Dear God, guard and bless everything that breathes; keep them from all evil and let them sleep in peace."

Memoirs of Childhood and Youth, 1924

❧

The only originality which I claim for myself is . . . that the human spirit in our time is capable of creating a new attitude of mind: an attitude based on ethics.

Nobel Peace Prize address, 1954

❧

The destiny of man has to fulfill itself in a thousand ways, so that goodness may be actualized. What every individual has to contribute remains his own secret. But we must all mutually share in the knowledge that our existence only attains its true value when we have experienced in ourselves the truth of the declaration: "He who loses his life shall find it."

Philosophy of Civilization, Part I, 1923

❧

What is Reverence for Life and how does it originate in us? If one clearly understands himself and his relations with the world, he must ever reflect on the novel which is fashioned from the many, perceptible elements of his consciousness and on the primal, immediate, and continually given elements of consciousness. Only in this way can he arrive at a rational worldview.

Out of My Life and Thought, 1931

Only after the Reformation did the idea gradually arise that we men and women in our own age must so understand the religion of Jesus that we endeavor to make the Kingdom of God a reality in this world. It is only through the idea of the Kingdom of God that religion enters into relationship with civilization.

"Busy Days in Lambaréné," article, 1934

❧

I do my work far from the world, in the forest, at the end of a river. I enjoy a certain solitude which gives me the strength to do my work. I have no vacation, no free day, no Sunday. But nevertheless I have the privilege of belonging in a way to myself.

Letter to Adlai Stevenson, 1956

❧

We must go back to the point where we can feel again the heroic in Jesus. Before that mysterious Person, who, in the form of his time, knew that he was creating upon the foundation of his life and death a moral world which bears his name, we must be forced to lay our faces in the dust, without daring even to wish to understand his nature.

The Mystery of the Kingdom of God, 1914

When I was an auxiliary preacher at St. Nicholas's Church, I asked the old ministers at the church to allow me to remain at the altar after the service and to spend ten or twelve minutes reading my selections from the Old or New Testament out loud in order to make people more familiar with the Bible. The ministers were kind enough to acquiesce, and both they and I were surprised that the congregation enjoyed it. After all, theoretically, we Protestants believe in the Bible, but we are unfamiliar with it because at services only the verses that the pastor wants to preach about are read aloud to the congregation. The worshipers greatly appreciated the reading of the Bible; some of them even complimented me by saying that they came more for the Bible reading than for my sermon.

Letter to the Reverend Willy Bremi, 1964

I studied Indian philosophy early on, when I was attending the University of Strasbourg, Alsace, even though no course was being given on that subject. Rabindranath Tagore became known as the great living Indian thinker. When I grew conversant with his teachings, they made a deep impact on me.

Letter to Asiatic Society, Calcutta, February 1965

❧

Any religion or philosophy which is not based on a respect for life is not a true religion or philosophy.

Letter to the Japanese Animal Society, 1961

❧

The doctrine of Reverence for Life is now being taught in many schools. It has made its way without a struggle. It was born in Lambaréné. That is why I feel so much at home here.

Letter to harpsichordist Alice Ehlers, 1963

❧

Educated or not educated, whoever is willing to think a little understands my philosophical books. For my philosophy is simple. It has only one subject, that we should become simpler and better human beings, that we should become more humane humans than we are.

Letter to harpsichordist Alice Ehlers, 1964

❧

Although I came to Gabon as a physician, I continued to be interested in philosophy and I believed that the main concern of philosophy is to make men better.

Letter to President Lyndon B. Johnson, 1962

❧

The elemental fact, present in our consciousness every moment of our existences, is: I am life that wills to live, in the midst of life that wills to live. The mysterious fact of my will to live is that I feel a mandate to behave with sympathetic concern toward all the wills to live which exist side by side with my own.

Address before the French Academy, 1952

❧

By ethical conduct toward all creatures, we enter into a spiritual relationship with the Universe. In the Universe, the will to live is in conflict with itself. In us, it seeks to be at peace with itself. In the Universe, the will to live is a fact; in us, it is a revelation.

Address before the French Academy, 1952

༈

We must think things out afresh and arrive at a philosophy of life that contains the ideals of true culture. If only we began again to reflect upon ethics and our spiritual relationship to the world, we would be on the road that leads from barbarism to culture.

"Ethical Culture," in The Teaching of Reverence for Life, 1963

༈

I know that you are all as convinced as I that in spite of suffering we need not doubt God's love and faithfulness. We are still heirs of his kingdom and still his children, and so we may rest assured that he will always lift us above misfortune. That is why our Lord says to us: "Blessed are those who suffer, for they shall be comforted."

"Creative Suffering," sermon preached on May 14, 1900

⁂

We never assume that reason and heart can walk effortlessly hand in hand. But the true heart is rational and the true reason has sensitivity. As we noticed, both heart and reason agree that in the last resort the good consists in elemental reverence of the enigma we call life, in reverence for all its manifestations, both great and small.

"Ethics of Compassion," sermon preached on February 23, 1919

⁂

Today the task is to get the mass of individuals to reclaim their spiritual heritage and so to regain the privilege they have renounced of thinking as free personalities. They must work themselves out of the condition of spiritual weakness and dependence to which they have brought themselves.

Interview with Melvin Arnold in Lambaréné, 1947

Under the influence of Christianity, ethics within philosophy acquire an enthusiasm never attained before. Under the influence of philosophy, on the other hand, the Christian ethic turns to the world and begins to consider what it is to mean and to achieve in this world.

Address before the French Academy, 1952

Whenever I was in complete despair, I thought of Goethe, who had imagined his Faust, in the end, busily regaining land from the sea where men might live and find nourishment. So Goethe stood beside me in the gloomy forest as the great smiling comforter who understood me.

Goethe Prize address, Frankfurt, 1928

Our real strength for the work we find every day anew is the realization of the grace which comes to us in that we are allowed to be active in the service of the mercy of Jesus.

"Busy Days in Lambaréné," article, 1934

There are native Christians who are in every respect thoroughly moral personalities; I meet one every day. It is Ojembo, the teacher in our boys' school, whose name means "a song"; I look upon him as one of the finest men that I know anywhere.

On the Edge of the Primeval Forest, 1921

What we call love is in its essence Reverence for Life. All material and spiritual values are values only insofar as they serve the maintenance of life at its highest level and the furtherance of life. Ethics are boundless in their domain and limitless in their demands. They are concerned with all living things that come within our sphere.

Indian Thought and Its Development, 1934

The greatest spirits among men have endeavored to unite thought and religion, because they judged it necessary for the spiritual welfare of man. In a time which must achieve reverence for spiritual truth, we carry on this effort. For us, the nuclear doctrine of Christianity is the Kingdom of God. Only a Christianity which is animated and ruled by the idea and the intent of the Kingdom of God is genuine. Only such a Christianity can give to mankind what it so desperately needs.

Letter to the International Society of Free Christianity, 1947

To me preaching was a necessity of my being. I felt it as something wonderful that I was allowed to address a congregation every Sunday about the deepest questions of life.

Out of My Life and Thought, 1931

Reverence for Life affords me my fundamental principle of morality, namely, that good consists in maintaining, assisting, and enhancing life and that to destroy, to harm, or to hinder life is evil. Affirmation of the world—that is affirmation of the will to live, which appears in phenomenal forms all around me—is only possible for me in that I give myself out for other life.

From a letter written shortly before his death, 1965

Until culture wakes up to its own mission and does something about it, let no one say a word against missions. Missionaries were the ones who stepped in the breach for our culture, for our civilization, for our society—and they did for other people what all the other agencies should have done.

"The Call to Mission," sermon preached on January 6, 1905

The fundamental fact of human awareness is this: "I am life that wills to live in the midst of life that wills to live." A thinking man feels compelled to approach all life with the same reverence he has for his own. Thus, all life becomes part of his own experience.

"Albert Schweitzer Speaks Out," article for World Book Yearbook, 1964

4 LOVE FOR ALL CREATION
. . . .
Human and Animal Rights

The struggle to maintain veracity is a basic element of spiritual life.

It is our task to unearth and proclaim once more the indestructible rights of man, rights which afford the individual the utmost possible freedom for his individuality in his own human group; human rights which guarantee protection to his existence and his personal dignity against every alien power to which he may become subject.

Philosophy of Civilization, Part 2, 1923

The human rights declaration was based not only on legal but also on moral grounds, and it is for moral reasons that we must make our stand against extinction. The fact that law is based on morality is the decisive thing in this case and must be brought to the force. Only if we keep stressing these facts can we fight the good fight, can we arouse public opinion—a public opinion that is common to all peoples.

Letter to Norman Cousins, 1959

Every man and woman who thinks simply and naturally cannot do otherwise than express love in action, not only on behalf of human beings, but also on behalf of all living things. We, no longer expecting the redemption of the whole creation from suffering as the outcome of the immediate end of the world, are compelled by the commandment of love contained in our hearts and thoughts, and proclaimed by Jesus, to give rein to our natural sympathy for animals. We are also compelled to help them and spare them suffering as far as it is in our power.

"Philosophy and the Movement for the Protection of Animals," article, 1935

Ethics cannot be based upon our obligations toward men, but they are complete and natural only when we feel this Reverence for Life and the desire to have compassion for and to help all creatures insofar as it is in our power. I think that this ethic will become more and more recognized because of its great naturalness and because it is the foundation of a true humanism toward which we must strive if our culture is to become truly ethical.

Letter to Elinore Barber, 1963

The spirit of humanity is a creative spirit and therefore we trust in it not only because it remains our hope in these times, but because it is able to fulfill its historic task.

The German Peace Prize address, 1951

The human spirit is not dead: It lives on in secret. It has come to believe that compassion, in which all ethics must take root, can only attain its full breadth and depth if it embraces all living creatures and does not limit itself to mankind. Ancient ethics had not this depth, this strength of conviction, but beside it there now stands a new ethic—that of respect for life, whose validity is more and more widely acknowledged.

Nobel Peace Prize address, 1954

My life is full of meaning to me. The life around me must be full of significance to itself. If I am to expect others to respect my life, then I must respect the other life I see, however strange it may be to mine. . . . Ethics in our Western world has hitherto been largely limited to the relations of man to man. But that is a limited ethics. We need a boundless ethics which will include the animals also.

The Philosophy of Civilization, Part 1, 1923

Thought cannot avoid the ethic of reverence and love for all life. It will abandon the old confined systems of ethics and be forced to recognize the ethics that knows no bounds. But on the other hand, those who believe in love for all creation must realize clearly the difficulties involved in the problem of a boundless ethic and must be resolved not to veil from man the conflicts in which this ethic will involve him, but allow him really to experience them. To think out in every implication the ethic of love for all creation—this is the difficult task which confronts our age.

"Philosophy and the Movement for the Protection of Animals," article, 1935

What does Reverence for Life say about the relations between man and the animal world? Whenever I injure any kind of life I must be quite certain that it is necessary. I must never go beyond the unavoidable, not even in apparently insignificant things. The farmer who has mowed down a thousand flowers in his meadow in order to feed his cows must be careful on his way home not to strike the head off a single flower by the side of the road in idle amusement, for he thereby infringes the law of life without being under the pressure of necessity.

The Philosophy of Civilization, Part I, 1929

Let us regard as valid only that which is compatible with humanity. . . . We hold high once more the sacred human rights, not those that the political rulers praise in their speeches and trample in their actions but the true ones. Once more we demand justice, not the one elaborated by lawyers deadened by juridical scholastics or that for which demagogues of all political shades shout themselves hoarse but a justice filled with the value of every human existence. The foundation of law is humanity.

Memoirs of Childhood and Youth, 1924

I am certain, and have always stressed, that the destination of mankind is to become more and more humane. The ideal of humanity has to be revived. Without this ideal we are lost human beings.

Letter to the Animal Defence League of Canada, 1965

While still a student, I resolved to devote my life until I was thirty to the office of preacher, to science, and to music. If by that time I should have done what I hoped in science and music, I would take a path of immediate service to my fellowman.

Memoirs of Childhood and Youth, 1924

The ethic of Reverence for Life prompts us to keep each other alert to what troubles us and to speak and act dauntlessly together in discharging the responsibility that we feel. It keeps us watching together for opportunities to bring some sort of help to animals in recompense for the great misery that men inflict upon them, and thus for a moment we escape from the incomprehensible horror of existence.

Philosophy of Civilization, Part 1, 1923

Whenever an animal is somehow forced into the service of men, every one of us must be concerned for any suffering it bears on that account. No one of us may permit any preventable pain to be inflicted, even though the responsibility for that pain is not ours. No one may appease his conscience by thinking that he would be interfering in something that does not concern him. No one may shut his eyes and think the pain, which is therefore not visible to him, is nonexistent.

Philosophy of Civilization, Part 2, 1923

❧

The exhibiting of trained animals I abhor. What an amount of suffering and cruel punishment the poor creatures have to endure in order to give a few moments of pleasure to men devoid of all thought and feeling.

Memoirs of Childhood and Youth, 1924

❦

When will we reach the point that hunting, the pleasure of killing animals for sport, will be regarded as a mental aberration? We must reach the point that killing for sport will be felt as a disgrace to our civilization.

"Man and Creature," in The Teaching of Reverence for Life, 1963

❦

To put an end by mercy killing to the suffering of a creature, when that suffering cannot be alleviated, is more ethical than to stand aloof from it.

Indian Thought and Its Development, 1934

⁂

Oh, this "noble" culture of ours! It speaks so piously of human dignity and human rights and then disregards this dignity and these rights of countless millions and treads them underfoot, only because they live overseas or because their skins are of different color or because they cannot help themselves.

"The Call to Mission," sermon preached on January 6, 1905

⁂

The fundamental rights of man are, first, the right to habitation; second, the right to move freely; third, the right to the soil and subsoil, and to the use of it; fourth, the right to freedom of labor and of exchange; fifth, the right to justice; sixth, the right to live within a natural national organization; and, seventh, the right to education.

"The Relations of the White and Colored Races,"
article for the Contemporary Review, 1928

White and nonwhite must strive toward the goal of meeting in an ethical spirit. Only then will true understanding be possible. Working toward the creation of this spirit constitutes a highly promising policy.

"My Message to Mankind," phonograph record, Lambaréné, 1964

Before the pile is lowered in the hole, I always look to see whether any ants or toads or other creatures have fallen into it. And if so, I take them out with my hands, that they may not be crushed by the pile or later killed by the pounding down of earth and stones.

On the Edge of the Primeval Forest, 1921

৯৫

Humanity has always needed ethical ideals to enable it to find the right path, that man may make the right use of the power he possesses. Today his power is increased a thousandfold. A thousandfold greater is now the need for man to possess ethical ideals to point the way.

"Religion and Modern Civilization,"
article for the Christian Century, 1934

৯৫

Our civilization lacks humane feeling. We are humans who are insufficiently humane! We must realize that and seek to find a new spirit.

Letter to Aida Flemming, founder of the Kindness Club, 1959

From the natives I buy a young fish eagle, which they have caught on a sandbank, in order to rescue it from their cruel hands. But now I must decide whether I shall let it starve, or whether I shall kill a certain number of small fish every day in order to keep it alive. I decide upon the latter course. But every day I find it rather hard to sacrifice—upon my own responsibility—one life for another.

Out of My Life and Thought, 1931

The sun of hope is not shining upon our paths. Night is still here, and our generation will not live to see the dawn of the new day. But if we have preserved our faith in that which must come, then stars will lighten our way and bring Light.

"The Future of Mankind," sermon preached on October 13, 1918

How are we to build a new humanity? Only by leading men toward a true, inalienable ethic of our own, which is capable of further development. But this goal cannot be reached unless countless individuals will transform themselves from blind men into seeing ones and begin to spell out the great commandment, which is: Reverence for Life.

"Reverence for Life," sermon preached on February 16, 1919

The spirit is not dead; it lives in isolation. It has overcome the difficulty of having to exist in a world out of harmony with its ethical character. It has come to realize that it can find no home other than in the basic nature of man. . . .

Nobel Peace Prize address, 1954

࿔

How few are the deeds done in the name of humanity as a whole. We must think and work in terms of man and of humanity. That is the important thing. That is the striking thing.

Interview with Melvin Arnold in Lambaréné, 1947

࿔

The ethical relationship of man to man is not something in and of itself, but part of a greater concept. The idea of Reverence for Life contains everything that expresses love, submission, compassion, the sharing of joy, and common striving for the good of all.

"Albert Schweitzer Speaks Out," article for World Book Yearbook, 1964

ॐ

So many people gave me something or were something to me without knowing it. . . . I always think that we all live, spiritually, by what others have given us in the significant hours of our life. These significant hours do not announce themselves as coming but arrive unexpected.

Memoirs of Childhood and Youth, 1924

ॐ

The great fault of all ethics hitherto has been that they believed themselves to have to deal only with the relations of man to man. In reality, however, the question is what is his attitude to the world and all life that comes within his reach. A man is ethical only when life, as such, is sacred to him, that of plants and animals as that of his fellow men, and when he devotes himself helpfully to all life that is in need of help. Only the universal ethic of the feeling of responsibility in an ever-widening sphere for all that lives—only that ethic can be founded in thought. The ethic of the relation of man to man is not something apart by itself: it is only a particular relation which results from the universal one. The ethic of Reverence for Life, therefore, comprehends within itself everything that can be described as love, devotion, and sympathy, whether in suffering, joy, or effort.

Out of My Life and Thought, 1931

So many people gave me something or were something to me without knowing it. . . . I always think that we all live, spiritually, by what others have given us in the significant hours of our life. These significant hours do not announce themselves as coming but arrive unexpected.

Memoirs of Childhood and Youth, 1924

୬ୡ

No right is more fundamental or more essential than that of the free disposal by a man of his labor. In the present condition of things, however, we are confronted from time to time by circumstances and conditions that seem to make it essential for the state to demand labor. The state has the right to impose taxes to be collected in money or in kind. Has it also the right to collect service in actual labor?

"The Relations of the White and Colored Races,"
article for the Contemporary Review, 1928

୬ୡ

A LANGUAGE OF SOUND

··

Music and the Arts

*The manifestations of strength, also of
spiritual strength, are mysterious.*

Joy, sorrow, tears, lamentation, laughter—to all these music gives voice, but in such a way that we are transported from the world of unrest to a world of peace, and see reality in a new way, as if we were sitting by a mountain lake and contemplating hills and woods and clouds in the tranquil and fathomless water.

Johann Sebastian Bach, 1908

❧

The work and the worry that fell to my lot through the practical interest I took in organ building made me sometimes wish that I had never troubled myself about it, but if I do not give it up, the reason is that the struggle for the good organ is to me part of the struggle for truth.

Out of My Life and Thought, 1931

❧

I have given much time and energy to the struggle for the true organ. Many a night I have spent over organ plans which had to be approved or revised. And I have undertaken many a journey in order to study the question of restoring or rebuilding an organ. . . . The hardest fights were those on behalf of preserving old organs. . . . The first old organ which I saved—with much trouble—was the excellent work of Silbermann at St. Thomas in Strasbourg. My friends used to say, "In the South he rescues old Africans, in the North old organs."

Out of My Life and Thought, 1931

Bach commands a language of sound. His music is a vehicle of recurring rhythmical motives, voicing peaceful happiness, living joy, intense pain, or misery sublimely met. The drive to express poetic and pictorial thoughts is the essence of music. Music is an invitation to the creative imagination of the hearer to make alive the feelings and the visions from which it derived. But this can only come to pass if he who speaks in the language of sound possesses the mysterious capacity of rendering thought clearly and vividly. On this point, Bach is the greatest among the great.

Out of My Life and Thought, 1931

Every artistic idea is complex in quality until the moment when it finds definite expression. Neither in painting nor in music nor in poetry is there such a thing as an absolute art that can be regarded as the norm, enabling us to brand all others as false, for in every artist there dwells another, who wishes to have his own say in the matter, the difference being that in one his activity is obtrusive, and in another hardly noticeable. Herein resides the whole distinction. Art in itself is neither painting nor poetry nor music, but an act of creation in which all three cooperate.

Johann Sebastian Bach, 1908

Music is an act of worship with Bach. His artistic activity and his personality are both based on his piety. If he is to be understood from any standpoint at all, it is from this. For him, art was religion and so had no concern with the world or with worldly success. It was an end in itself. Bach includes religion in the definition of art in general. All great art, even secular, is in itself religious in his eyes; for him the tones do not perish but ascend to God like praise too deep to utter.

Johann Sebastian Bach, 1908

We are led astray by the "concert organ." What is a concert organ? Are there two kinds of organ? Or is there only the best organ, and is this not the church organ? What would old Bach say if he heard our distinction between an organist and an organ virtuoso? Is there something better than a good organist who remains invisible behind his instrument, letting it speak only to the glory of God?

The Art of Organ Building and Organ Playing in Germany and France, 1906

Who will give us back our old organs which in our blindness we denied? Who will replace the old master organ builders who were compelled to renounce their vocation during a senseless period of commercialized organ building? The words of Lao-tze are relevant: "He who wins should act as though celebrating his own funeral."

The Art of Organ Building and Organ Playing in Germany and France, 1906

The sense of almost all the answers is that the master of organ building must be so placed that he can serve his art without worry about his living, and with the assurance of a modest income; without having to wear himself out in a price war, and without having to submit himself unconditionally to the whims of an expert. If things go on as they are, in twenty to forty years organ building in most countries will be so ruined, artistically and economically, that it will have ceased to exist as an artistic handcraft.

The Questionnaire on Organ Construction, 1909

The test of every organ, the best and only test, is Bach's organ music. Let one apply this test artistically to organ building, instead of trying to imagine how Bach would throw his peruke in the air for joy over our pistons, and then after catching it again, set off to find out from one of our modern organ virtuosi how on the modern organ one can bring everything out of his music.

The Art of Organ Building and Organ Playing in Germany and France, 1906

Beethoven and Wagner poetize in music, Bach paints. And Bach is a dramatist, but just in the sense that the painter is. He does not paint successive events but seizes upon the pregnant moment that contains the whole event for him and depicts this in music.

Johann Sebastian Bach, 1908

The work of the objective artist is not impersonal; it is superpersonal. It is as if he felt but a single impulse, namely, to display definitively in a unique perfection what he finds in life. It is not he who lives—the spirit of the time lives in him. All the artistic movements, desires, creations, aspirations, and errors of his own generation and of the previous ones are comprehended and worked out in him.

Johann Sebastian Bach, 1908

The part of a work of art that is perceptible by the senses is in reality only the mediator between two active efforts of the imagination. All art speaks in signs and symbols. No one can explain how it happens that the artist can waken to life in us the existence that he has seen and lives through. No artistic speech is the adequate expression of what it represents; its vital force comes from what is unspoken in it.

Johann Sebastian Bach, 1908

Bach himself could not think of playing his organ works quickly, as the mechanism of his manuals was difficult to play. I have myself in Alsace played organs of Silbermann of the eighteenth century on which the pressing down of the keys was a real effort. Another impediment is the fact that the keys in these old organs go down twice as deep as in modern ones. An old great organ, on which all difficulties of the old mechanisms can be experienced, is in Leewarden in the north of Holland; but what wonderful sound it has!

Letter to the organist Gardner Evans, 1942

The harpsichord is a historically interesting instrument, which is essential in performing certain types of music and should be properly cultivated by us. But it was not Bach's ideal; he rather sought an instrument on which he could play "cantabile" and therefore came back again and again to the clavichord.

Letter to the harpsichordist Alice Ehlers, 1928

ॐ

My only relaxation is practicing on the organ. I do this passionately in every free moment. A whole series of preludes and fugues have been thoroughly reworked and are now more profound and better crafted. At times I think: What will it be like when you perform this on a good organ for Siegfried Ochs!

Letter to Siegfried Ochs, Philharmonic Choir, Berlin, 1927

ॐ

My sole relaxation is practicing the organ on my pedal piano. At the moment I am working on Cesar Franck's last organ works. I assume that you relax with your violin. . . .

Letter to Albert Einstein, February 20, 1955

Only he who sinks himself in Bach's emotional world, who lives and thinks with him, and who is as simple and modest as he, can rightly bring Bach's music to the listener. If the director and the performer are not consecrated in thought and mood, they cannot communicate effectively to the hearer.

Johann Sebastian Bach, 1908

Wherever I could, after the appearance of my Bach book, I talked about the round violin bow with violinists of reputation and sought to win them to this project. But they were all averse to it. Why? They were all convinced that the tone that would be produced by the moderately stretched bow would not please our ears, accustomed as they are to the intensive tone of the violin. To justify this conviction they usually referred to the tone that one gets if one loosens the hairs on an ordinary straight bow, puts the stick under the violin, lays the hairs on the strings, and holding them and the stick with the right hand draws the hairs over the strings with the reversed and completely relaxed bow. They forget that the hairs of the round bow are never as completely relaxed as they are in this violinist's trick.

"The Round Violin Bow," article, 1933

ॐ

It has a significance for all future times that the symphony of Christianity began with a tremendous dissonance between faith and thought, which later resolved itself into a harmony.

The Mysticism of Paul the Apostle, 1931

I cried over my lot in secret for hours and hours. I felt as if I were being torn away from Nature. To the enthusiasm roused in me by the beauties of Nature as I learned to know them on my walks to and from Münster, I tried to give expression in poetry, but I never got further than the first two or three rhymes. Once or twice too I tried to sketch the hill with the old castle on it which rose from the other side of the valley, but that too was a failure. . . . Only in musical improvisation have I ever felt myself—as I do still—to have any creative ability.

Memoirs of Childhood and Youth, 1924

Bach himself was not conscious of the extraordinary greatness of his work. He was aware only of his admitted mastery of the organ and clavier and counterpoint. But he never dreamed that his works alone, not those of the men all round him, would remain visible to the coming generations. If it is one of the signs of the great creative artist, born before his time, that he waits for "his day" and wears himself out in the waiting, then was Bach neither great nor born before his time. No one was less conscious than he that his work was ahead of his epoch. In this respect he stands, perhaps, highest among all creative artists; his immense strength functioned without self-consciousness, like the force of nature; and for this reason it is as cosmic and copious as these.

Johann Sebastian Bach, 1908

If it is possible for Your Majesty to pass through Gunsbach this year, then my organ and I would be profoundly happy and we would strain to do our best. I have prepared Franck's second chorale for Columbia [Records]; I have always been moved by the depth of this music, which I came to appreciate when it was published several months after the maestro's death.

Letter to Queen Elisabeth of Belgium, July 8, 1952

The Brandenburg concertos are the purest revelation of Bach's polyphonic style. Neither on the organ nor on the clavier could he have worked out the architectonic structure of a piece with such vitality. The orchestra alone permits absolute freedom in the employment and grouping of obbligato voices.

Johann Sebastian Bach, 1908

6 THE REIGN OF PEACE

War and Peace

We all have to struggle to be willing to become truly peaceful.

May those who have in their hands the fate of the nations take care to avoid whatever may worsen our situation and make it more dangerous. And may they take to heart the words of the apostle Paul: "If it be possible, as much as lieth in you, live peaceably with all men." His words are valid not only for individuals but for whole nations as well. May the nations, in their efforts to keep peace in being, go to the farthest limits of possibility so that the spirit of man shall be given time to develop and grow strong—and time to act.

Nobel Peace Prize address, 1954

The awareness that we are all human beings has become lost in war and politics. We have reached the point of regarding each other only as members of a people either allied with us or against us and our approach—prejudice, sympathy, or antipathy—are all conditioned by that. Now we must rediscover the fact that we—all together—are human beings, and that we must strive to concede to each other what moral capacity we have.

"Peace or Atomic War?" speech, 1958

If negotiations on disarmament are held, not as a preliminary to the renunciation of nuclear arms but as a result of it, they would have a much larger meaning. They would be a big step in the direction of finally liquidating the confused situation that followed from the Second World War. Disarmament and all questions leading to a stable situation—such as, for example, the reunification of East and West Germany—could be discussed much better after agreement had been reached on the renunciation of atomic weapons. A later conference could also deal with many issues left unresolved in the peace treaties after the Second World War.

"Peace or Atomic War?" speech, 1958

My hope is that, by the gravity of the situation created by the resumption of tests, men throughout the world will understand that they must arrive at a solution to the problem of the terrible danger in which humanity is placed. They can no longer let things go, as they have been doing. We must understand that we are risking the terrible catastrophe in which humanity will perish.

Letter to Norman Cousins, 1961

If humanity is to bring us peace in the world, it must also represent what is good for ALL peoples. This is more important today than at any other time because it is in our time that those nations which have hitherto had no share in the higher civilization—the under-developed nations—are becoming independent states in their own right. Thus the world view is totally changing.

German Peace Prize address, 1951

The end of further experiments with atom bombs would be like the early sun rays of hope which suffering humanity is longing for.

"A Declaration of Conscience," speech, 1957

๕

An urgent necessity for the world is that the atomic powers agree as soon as possible on disarmament under effective international control. The possibility of such disarmament negotiations should not be made questionable by unnecessary appeals for international verification of the discontinuance of testing. Only when the states agree not to carry out tests any more can promising negotiations about disarmament and peace take place.

Letter to President John F. Kennedy, 1962

๕

All weapons which produce radioactivity, even those which are being praised as clean, have to be looked on as opposed to the *Volkerrecht* [international law] and must be abandoned.

Letter to Norman Cousins, 1958

Everywhere in the world people fear for peace and . . . the fate of mankind is in the balance. But where does this fear—this confusion in which we find ourselves—stem from? It stems from the power gained by the progress in man's knowledge and his increased technical capabilities.

German Peace Prize address, 1951

That the reign of peace will eventually come to pass . . . has been discounted as "utopian," but the situation today is such that it must in one way or another become reality if humanity is not to perish.

Nobel Peace Prize address, 1954

❦

I, on my part, have been able to raise the coward's mask, because I had the privilege, as winner of the Nobel Peace Prize, to speak with absolute liberty about all questions pertaining to world peace, via Radio Oslo, particularly about the fact that, because atomic weapons are a violation of international law, this means a threat to the continuation of such armament.

Letter to Pablo Casals, 1958

❦

In my heart I carry the hope I may somehow be able to contribute to the peace of the world. This I know has always been your own deepest wish. We both share the conviction that humanity must find a way to control the weapons which now menace the very existence of life on earth.

Letter to President Dwight D. Eisenhower, 1957

꙳

Today there is an absence of thinking which is characterized by a contempt for life. We waged war for questions which, through reason, might have been solved. No one won. The war killed millions of men and brought suffering and death to millions of innocent animals. Why? Because we did not possess the highest rationality of Reverence for Life.

"The Ethics of Reverence for Life," article, 1936

꙳

Today, once again, we live in a period that is marked by the absence of peace; today, once again, nations feel themselves menaced by other nations; today, once again, we must concede to each the right to defend himself with the terrible weapons which are now at our disposal. . . .

Nobel Peace Prize address, 1954

ॐ

Reason never complacently rests in faith, for true peace comes from what happens with our own will, from what it seeks. The peace of God can be ours only if our will finds peace in the infinite.

"The Peace of God," sermon preached on March 9, 1913

ॐ

I am well aware that what I have had to say on the problem of peace is not essentially new. It is my profound conviction that the solution lies in our rejecting war for an ethical reason, namely, that war makes us guilty of the crime of inhumanity. . . .

Nobel Peace Prize address, 1954

Only when an ideal of peace is born in the minds of the peoples will the institutions set up to maintain this peace effectively fulfill the function expected of them.

Nobel Peace Prize address, 1954

What really matters is that we should all of us realize that we are guilty of inhumanity. The horror of this realization should shake us out of our lethargy so that we can direct our hopes and our intentions to the coming of an era in which war will have no place. This hope and this will can have but one aim: to attain, through a change in spirit, that superior reason which will dissuade us from misusing the power at our disposal.

Nobel Peace Prize address, 1954

Few governments take seriously the horrible effects of atomic explosions and even of test explosions, and many are inclined to go along with this inhumanity. That is why I have entered the struggle against nuclear weapons, although I am almost too old to take part. But I can still accomplish something—since as a recipient of the Nobel Peace Prize I have the privilege of speaking in full freedom over Radio Oslo on all matters concerning peace, including the danger of nuclear weapons to the world.

Letter to Polish doctor, no date

Man has become a superman. He is a superman not only because he has at his command innate physical forces, but because, thanks to science and technical advancement, he now controls the latent forces of nature and can bring them, if he wishes, into play. . . . But this superman suffers from a fatal imperfection of mind. He has not raised himself to that superhuman level of reason which should correspond to the possession of superhuman strength.

Nobel Peace Prize address, 1954

Kant published, with the title *Towards Perpetual Peace*, a work containing rules which were to be observed with a view to lasting peace whenever treaties of peace were concluded. It was a mistake. Rules for treaties of peace, however well intentioned and however ably drawn up, can accomplish nothing. Only such thinking as establishes the sway of the mental attitude of Reverence for Life can bring to mankind perpetual peace.

Philosophy of Civilization, Part 2, 1923

That radioactive elements created by us are found in nature is an astounding event in the history of the earth and of the human race. To fail to consider its importance and its consequences would be a folly for which humanity would have to pay a terrible price. We are committing a folly in thoughtlessness. It must not happen that we do not pull ourselves together before it is too late. We must muster the insight, the seriousness, and the courage to leave folly and to face reality.

"A Declaration of Conscience," speech, 1957

As the recipient of the Nobel Peace Prize, I am tempted, as I have written to you, to talk about the problem of peace in our time. I know that this is a very thorny issue, but perhaps it would be worthwhile trying to treat it in a thorough manner by seeking to envision how to get humanity today to truly want peace and how we could try to bring peace about. If you have no objections to my tackling such a vast and topical issue, I will do so.

Letter to Gunnar Jahn, Nobel Prize Committee, November 30, 1953

❧

Any policy that ignores the fact of the horrible destructive power of today's nuclear arms is nothing but nonsensical adventurism. We have no choice but to recognize that in order to lead a humane existence again, we must mutually resolve to abolish atomic weapons, on which we have already spent and would like to continue spending billions upon billions.

Letter to Jack Anderson, "Parade Magazine," Washington, D.C., 1963

The yearning for peace is great in the hearts of mankind today. For them, a revelation of the spirit of peace will be an experience with unforeseeable consequences. It is only through the miracle of awakening the spirit of peace in mankind that it can be kept from perishing. May it be granted to us that the efforts toward avoiding war are successful and that in the time that is thereby given us we can make the spirit of peace so powerful that it will start to become the Kingdom of God in ourselves and in the world.

"What Mankind Needs Most at This Time," article, February 1952

7   A SPIRIT OF HUMANITY

Global Order

A spirit of true humanity has to arise among us if we are not to perish through the spirit of inhumanity.

Our task is to raise our voices permanently in order to waken those who are asleep and to build up a public opinion which is capable of bearing pressure upon the governments.

Letter to Norman Cousins, 1959

❧

I believe that there is reason for hope. Hope is there like a small band of light on the sky before the sunrise. There begins to stir in the world a new spirit, a spirit of humanity. The terrible thing was that we fell into inhumanity without knowing it. And because the new spirit begins to stir there is hope, for the spirit is the great transforming power.

Letter to lieutenant in U.S. Navy, 1952

❧

I believe that all of us have something in us that illumines our own vision and our understanding of others, and that we are all a candle for others. It has been my experience that one small act can take possession of us suddenly to move and lead us.

Paris interview, 1959

❧

The fundamental principle of morality is respect for life. Good is: to know pity, to help others conserve their life, and to spare them suffering. Evil is: to ignore compassion and to fail to be involved with all kinds of creatures, to cause them to suffer and to die. The mysterious feeling of respect for life awakens in us when, in meditation upon ourselves and the world, we reach true understanding of ourselves. It brings us to devote ourselves to other creatures and to recognize, therefore, those moments of rejoicing which transform us in our pilgrimage on earth.

From a telegram, 1953

❧

We find ourselves in a new movement of thought. In a movement where, through science and through the searching of our hearts, everything has become mysterious. Science has led us from knowledge to knowledge but also from mystery to mystery. Mystery alone can lead us on to true spirituality, to accept and be filled with the mystery of life in our existence.

Joseph Lemaire Prize address, 1959

Our propaganda is passed on from man to man; its strength is that it represents what is true and sensible. Our propaganda has dignity. It works with simple means; it is noble. This we may not abandon and we must not ever adjust to a propaganda which uses any available means. We are prophets of the truth who can save the world.

Letter to Bertrand Russell, 1962

We cannot dictate anything to the United Nations. It is an autonomous body and has to find in itself the incentive and feeling of responsibility to try to prevent threatening disasters.

Letter to Albert Einstein, 1955

The two autobiographical works, *Memoirs of Childhood and Youth* and *Out of My Life and Thought,* are very dear to my heart, for they present the philosophy of humanitarianism in a popular way. The idea of spiritual solidarity with the world through Reverence for Life is the goal of everything I write and do. It is only by developing this spiritual civilization that the nations can behave differently toward one another. We all have to work together toward this new civilization, no matter what nation we belong to. Through these efforts we will move from the road of darkness to the road of life.

Letter to the Serbian Book Association, 1958

At last the ray of light is visible in the darkness in which mankind is seeking its path; this glimmer gives us hope that the darkness will yield to the light. The East-West pact that bans nuclear testing in the atmosphere and under water is one of the greatest events in world history. When I heard about the Moscow agreement, I thought of my friend Einstein, with whom I was allied in the battle against nuclear arms. When he died in Princeton, he was in despair.

Letter to President John F. Kennedy, 1963

The spirit of humanity . . . refers not only to its fellowman but encompasses everything in its domain. It needs no knowledge of life and the world, other than knowing that everything which exists is life, and of recognizing that we must regard with the greatest reverence all life as being of the most precious and irreplaceable value.

German Peace Prize address, 1951

Only to the extent in which the peoples of the world foster within themselves the ideal of peace will those institutions whose object is the preservation of that peace be able to function as we expect, and hope, that they will.

Nobel Peace Prize address, 1954

Never, in our earlier meeting in Europe, would we have imagined that one day we would together descend in the world arena to fight against those who constitute the greatest danger in the world.

Letter to Pablo Casals, 1958

&

May it be given to us both to see the day when the world's people will realize that the fate of all humanity is now at stake, and that it is urgently necessary to make the bold decisions that can deal adequately with the agonizing situation in which the world now finds itself.

Letter to President Dwight D. Eisenhower, 1957

&

How ghastly what is going on in the world! Helplessly one must watch as people who have done no wrong are delivered into the hands of their torturers. . . .

Letter to harpsichordist Alice Ehlers, 1938

I have, as you know, something very beautiful in my life: that my philosophy of humaneness is making its way in the world and means something to people. It succeeds through its own strength because it is true and brings a new spirit into our sad era.

Letter to harpsichordist Alice Ehlers, 1963

Mankind has the desire for a deeper and nobler civilization. There is a prospect that it will be achieved. And I have helped to push it ahead so that it may come about.

Letter to harpsichordist Alice Ehlers, 1964

❧

The only possible way out of the present chaos is for us to adopt a worldview which will bring us once more under that control of the ideals of true civilization which are contained in it.

Out of My Life and Thought, 1931

❧

Radioactive clouds resulting from a war between East and West would imperil humanity everywhere. . . . At all costs it must be prevented.

"Peace or Atomic War?" speech, 1958

&

At the present time when violence, clothed in life, dominates the world more cruelly than it ever has before, I still remain convinced that truth, love, peaceableness, meekness, and kindness are the powers which can master all other violence.

Memoirs of Childhood and Youth, 1924

&

What do we mean when we speak of *ethics,* in a word borrowed from the Greek, and *morality,* in a word from the Latin? We mean right human conduct. The assumption is that we should be concerned not only with our own welfare but also with that of others, and with that of human society as a whole.

Address before the French Academy, 1952

❧

How much farther along would we be if men showed some concern for other forms of life and renounced all the evils they inflict upon so many living creatures from sheer thoughtlessness. We must in our time make it our special task to struggle against the antihuman traditions and inhuman emotions that are still too much in our midst.

Address before the French Academy, 1952

❧

The more we act in accordance with the principle of Reverence for Life, the more we are gripped by the desire to preserve and benefit life. The principle of Reverence for Life includes an elemental sense of responsibility to which we must submit with all our being. There are forces active within that principle which cause us to refine our individual, social, and political attitudes.

"Ethical Culture," in The Teaching of Reverence for Life, 1963

The basic significance of all difficulty is that it reorients us from the external to the spiritual. The meaning and purpose of the world remain to a large extent inexplicable. But one thing is clear: the purpose of all events is spiritual.

"The Future of Mankind," sermon preached on October 13, 1918

❧

Reverence for human suffering and human life, for the smallest and most insignificant, must be the inviolable law to rule the world from now on. We must recognize that only a deep-seated change of heart, spreading from one man to another, can achieve such a thing in this world.

"Sacrifice of Others," sermon preached on December 1, 1918

❧

We feel that it is not right to be permanently preoccupied with our own well-being; the welfare of others and of human society in general must become part of our responsibility. The first step toward a development of this ethical principle is marked by an extension of this solidarity with our fellow creatures.

Address before the French Academy, October 1952

❧

The positive way of looking at things agrees with our natural sentiment; the negative one does not. The affirmative attitude invites us to make the world our home and dedicate our lives to action; a negative attitude leaves us as strangers in this world and dooms us to inactivity.

Address before the French Academy, October 1952

❧

One truth stands firm. All that happens in world history rests on something spiritual. If the spiritual is strong, it creates world history. If it is weak, it suffers world history. The question is, shall we make world history or only suffer it passively?

From the lectures "Religion in Modern Civilization," Oxford, 1934

Whereas the thoughtless modern world walks aimlessly about in ideals of knowledge, skills, and power, the goal of true and profound thought is the spiritual and ethical perfection of man. This requires a new ethical civilization that seeks peace and renounces war. Only the kind of thinking dominated by reverence for life can bring lasting peace to our world.

"Albert Schweitzer Speaks Out," article for World Book Yearbook, 1964

We must never permit the voice of humanity within us to be silenced. It is man's sympathy with all creatures that first makes him truly a man.

"The Revival of Falconry," article, March 1932

❧

There must indeed arise a philosophy profounder and more living than our own and endowed with greater spiritual and ethical force. In this terrible period through which mankind is passing, from the East and from the West we must all keep a lookout for the coming of this more perfect and more powerful form of thought which will conquer the hearts of individuals and compel whole peoples to acknowledge its sway. It is for this that we must strive.

Indian Thought and Its Development, Foreword, 1934

❧

What do our people and nations think about when they gaze across the sea? Of countries to be taken under their so-called protection or otherwise annexed? Of what they might siphon out of the country, always to their advantage?

"The Call to Mission," sermon preached on January 6, 1905

৵৻

We are robber states. And where are the people in our civilized states who will undertake long-term, selfless labor to educate other peoples and bring them the blessings of our culture? Where are the workmen, tradesmen, teachers, professors, and doctors who will go to these countries and work there to achieve the blessings of culture? What efforts does our society make in that direction? None at all. Only a few poor missionaries with all their limitations have undertaken a work that our whole society should have been eager to do.

"The Call to Mission," sermon preached on January 6, 1905

৵৻

The ethic of Reverence for Life is the ethic of love widened into universality.

Out of My Life and Thought, 1931

❧

The main thing is that India and the rest of the world are getting closer and closer to a deep ethical civilization, bringing an era in which no more wars will be fought and no more nuclear arms will be built.

Letter to Prime Minister Lal Bahadur Shastri, November 29, 1964

❧

There is this one hope: we must return to the main road, from which we have wandered. . . . We must substitute the power of understanding the truth that is really true, for propaganda; a noble kind of patriotism which aims at ends that are worthy of the whole of mankind, for the patriotism current today; a humanity with a common civilization, for idolized nationalisms; a restored faith in the civilized state, for a society which lacks true idealism; a unifying ideal of civilized man, for the condition into which we have plunged; a concern with the processes and ideals of true civilization, for a preoccupation with the transient problems of living; a faith in the possibility of progress, for a mentality stripped of all true spirituality.

My conviction has not changed. These tasks are our tasks today.

In response to question about hope for the future, interview with Melvin Arnold in Lambaréné, 1947

Biographical Time Line

1875	January 14, born in Kaysersberg, Alsace. During his first year, family moved to Gunsbach.
1880–84	Attended village school in Gunsbach.
1884–85	Attended Realschule in nearby Münster in preparation for Gymnasium.
1885–93	Attended Gymnasium in Mulhausen.
1893	October, first sojourn in Paris. Studied organ with Widor.
1893–98	Studied theology and philosophy at the University of Strasbourg.
1894–95	Military service.
1896	Decided to devote life to service of humanity, beginning at age thirty.
1898	May 6, passed first theology examination before faculty. First publication: *Eugene Munch, 1857–1898*.
1898–99	Second sojourn in Paris. Again studied under Widor.
1899	April–July, studied philosophy and organ in Berlin. July, received Ph.D. at Strasbourg. *The Religious Philosophy of Kant* (*Die Religionsphilosophie Kants*) published in December.

1900	July 21, obtained licentiate degree in theology, Strasbourg. September 23, ordained as a regular curate, St. Nicolai, Strasbourg.
1901	*The Problem of the Lord's Supper* (*Das Abendmahlsproblem auf Grund der wissenschaftlichen Forschung des 19. Jahrhunderts und der historischen Berichte*) published. *The Mystery of the Kingdom of God* (*Das Messianitäts und Leidensgeheimnis*) published. May–September, provisional appointment at St. Thomas Theological Seminary, Strasbourg.
1903	October, appointed principal of the Theological Seminary.
1905	*J. S. Bach le musicien-poete* published in Paris. October 13, informed family and friends of decision to study medicine and to serve in Africa. October, resigned post at theological seminary.
1905–12	Medical studies, University of Strasbourg.
1906	*The Art of Organ Building and Organ Playing in Germany and France* (*Deutsche und Französische Orgelbaukunst und Orgelkunst*) and *The Quest of the Historical Jesus* (*Von Reimarus zu Wrede: eine Geschichte der Leben-Jesu-Forschung*) published.
1908	*J. S. Bach,* the German edition published.

1909	*Internationales Regulativ für Orgelbau* published after participating in the Third Congress of the International Music Society in Vienna.
1911	Published *Paul and His Interpreters* (*Geschichte der Paulinischen Forschung*). December, passed his medical examinations.
1912	June 18, married Helene Bresslau. First two volumes of Bach's *Complete Organ Works* published, with C. M. Widor.
1913	February, granted Dr.Med. *Psychiatric Study of Jesus* published. Volumes 3–5 of Bach's *Complete Organ Works* published. March 26, departed for Lambaréné with his wife. Arrived April 16.
1913–17	First sojourn in Lambaréné.
1914	August–November, interned as enemy alien at Lambaréné.
1915	September, concept of Reverence for Life came to him during Ogowe River journey.
1917–18	September 1917, transferred with Mrs. Schweitzer to France. Internment in Bordeaux, Garaison, and St. Remy.
1918	July, returned to Alsace in an exchange of prisoners.
1919–21	Again served at St. Nicolai and as a doctor in the Strasbourg City Hospital.

1919	January 14, daughter Rhena born, on his birthday. December, receives invitation from Archbishop Söderblom to deliver some lectures in Upsala (Sweden).
1920	In Sweden for lectures and concerts to raise money for Lambaréné. Awarded honorary doctorate in divinity, University of Zurich (Switzerland).
1921	*On the Edge of the Primeval Forest* (*Zwischen Wasser und Urwald*) published.
1921–22	Lectures and concerts in Switzerland, England, Sweden, and Denmark.
1923	*The Philosophy of Civilization* (*Kulturphilosophie*) published. *Christianity and the Religions of the World* (*Das Christentum und die Weltreligionen*) published.
1924	*Memoirs of Childhood and Youth* (*Aus meiner Kindheit und Jugendzeit*) published.
1924–27	Second sojourn in Lambaréné (April 1924–July 1927), this time without Mrs. Schweitzer.
1925	*More from the Primeval Forest*, Part 1, (*Mitteilungen aus Lambaréné*, Part 1) published.
1926	*More from the Primeval Forest*, Part 2, (*Mitteilungen aus Lambaréné*, Part 2) published.
1927	January 21, moved hospital to new site two miles upstream.

1927–29	Lectures in Sweden, Denmark, Holland, Great Britain, Czechoslovakia, and Switzerland. Concerts in Germany. Presented honorary degree of doctor of philosophy, University of Prague.
1928	*More from the Primeval Forest,* Part 3, (*Mitteilungen aus Lambaréné,* Part 3) published.
1929–32	Third sojourn in Africa (December 1929– February 1932). Mrs. Schweitzer joined him until Easter 1930.
1929	*Selbstdarstellung* published. Awarded honorary doctorates in theology and philosophy, University of Edinburgh.
1930	*The Mysticism of Paul the Apostle* (*Die Mystik des Apostels Paulus*) published.
1931	*Out of My Life and Thought* (*Aus meinem Leben und Denken*) published. Awarded honorary doctorate in music, University of Edinburgh.
1932–33	February 1932–April 1933, in Europe for lectures and concerts. March 22, 1932, Goethe Gedenkrede (Centennial Celebration of Goethe's Death), Frankfurt. Awarded honorary doctorate in theology from Oxford and honorary LL.D. from St. Andrews.
1933–34	Fourth sojourn in Africa (April 1933–January 1934), again without Mrs. Schweitzer.

1934–35	In Europe. October 1934, Hibbert Lectures, Manchester College, Oxford. November, Gifford Lectures, Edinburgh, resulting in separate book on *Indian Thought and Its Development* (*Die Weltanschauung der Indischen Denker*), published in same year.
1935	Fifth sojourn in Lambaréné (February–August), again without Mrs. Schweitzer.
1935–37	In Europe (September 1935–February 1937). Second series of Gifford Lectures. Lectures and concerts in England. Recorded Bach organ music for Columbia.
1936	*African Hunting Stories* (*Afrikanische Jagdgeschichten*) published in book form.
1937–39	Sixth sojourn in Lambaréné (February 1937–January 1939), without Mrs. Schweitzer.
1938	*From My African Notebook* (*Afrikanische Geschichten*) published.
1939	February, arrived in Europe; returned immediately to Lambaréné because of danger of war.
1939–49	Seventh sojourn in Lambaréné (March 1939–October 1949). Mrs. Schweitzer joined him from 1941 to 1946.
1948	*The Jungle Hospital* (*Das Spital im Urwald*) and *Goethe: Two Addresses* published.

1948–49	October 1948–October 1949, mostly in Europe. July 1949, Goethe Bicentennial Convocation in Aspen, Colorado. July 11, awarded honorary LL.D., University of Chicago. *Goethe: Drie Reden* published.
1949–51	Eighth sojourn in Lambaréné (October 1949–June 1951). Mrs. Schweitzer joined him until June 1950.
1950	*Goethe: Vier Reden* published. *A Pelican Tells About His Life* (*Ein Pelikan erzahlt aus seinem Leben*) published in book form.
1951	July, returned to Europe. Recorded for Columbia. September 16, Peace Prize of the German Book Publishers. December 3, elected to the French Academy.
1951–52	Ninth sojourn in Lambaréné (December 1951–July 1952).
1952	July–December 1952, in Europe for lectures and concerts. September, awarded Paracelsus Medal by the German Medical Society. October, speech before the French Academy. Received Prince Carl Medal, grand medal of the Swedish Red Cross. Installed as a member of the Swedish Royal Academy of Music and awarded an honorary doctorate of theology by the University of Marburg.

1952–54	Tenth sojourn in Lambaréné (December 1952–June 1954).
1953	October, awarded the Nobel Peace Prize for 1952. Awarded honorary degree by University of Kapstadt.
1954	June–December 1954, in Europe. Volume 6 of Bach's *Complete Organ Works* published with Edouard Nies-Berger. November 4, Nobel Peace Prize speech, "The Problem of Peace in the World of Today."
1954–55	Eleventh sojourn in Lambaréné (December 1954–July 1955). January 14, 1955, 80th birthday celebrated in Lambaréné.
1955	July–December 1955, in Europe. Received Order of Merit in London; Order pour le Merite, Germany; and honorary Dr.Jur., Cambridge University.
1955–57	Twelfth sojourn in Lambaréné (December 1955–June 1957). Mrs. Schweitzer with him until May 22, 1957. April 23, 1957, first nuclear test ban broadcast. June 1, Helene Schweitzer-Bresslau died in Zurich.
1957	June 21–December 4, in Europe. Visited Switzerland and Germany.
1957–59	Thirteenth sojourn in Lambaréné (December 1957–August 1959).

1958	April 28, 29, 30, three addresses over Norwegian radio about nuclear war. Published as *Peace or Atomic War?* (*Friede oder Atomkrieg?*). Awarded honorary M.D., University of Münster. Awarded honorary Th.D., Tübingen.
1959	March 23, awarded Sonning Prize in Copenhagen for "work to the benefit of European culture."
1959	August–December 1959, in Europe. September 29, accepted Sonning Prize in Copenhagen. November 18, awarded Joseph Lemaire Prize in Brussels. December, final departure for Lambaréné.
1960	January 14, 85th birthday celebrated in Lambaréné.
1963	*Die Lehre der Ehrfurcht vor dem Leben* (*The Teaching of Reverence for Life*) published.
1965	January 14, 90th birthday celebrated in Lambaréné. September 4, died in Lambaréné.

Writings of Albert Schweitzer

1911	*Geschichte der Paulinischen Forschung* (*Paul and His Interpreters*, 1912)
1912	First two volumes of J. S. Bach's *Complete Organ Works* (with C. M. Widor)
1913	*Die Psychiatrische Beurteilung Jesu* (*Psychiatric Study of Jesus*, 1948) *Geschichte der Leben-Jesu-Forschung* (second edition of *The Quest of the Historical Jesus*, 1922) Volumes 3–5 of Bach's *Complete Organ Works* (again with C. M. Widor)
1921	*Zwischen Wasser und Urwald* (*On the Edge of the Primeval Forest*, 1922)
1923	*Kulturphilosophie* (*The Philosophy of Civilization*, 1923) *Das Christentum und die Weltreligionen* (*Christianity and the Religions of the World*, 1923)
1924	*Aus meiner Kindheit und Jugendzeit* (*Memoirs of Childhood and Youth*, 1924)
1925	*Mitteilungen aus Lambaréné*, I (*More from the Primeval Forest*, Part 1, 1931)
1926	*Mitteilungen aus Lambaréné*, II (*More from the Primeval Forest*, Part 2, 1931)
1928	*Mitteilungen aus Lambaréné*, III (*More from the Primeval Forest*, Part 3, 1931)
1929	*Selbstdarstellung*

Posthumously

1966	*Strassburger Predigten* (*Reverence for Life*, 1969)
1967	*Reich Gottes und Christentum* (*The Kingdom of God and Primitive Christianity*, 1968)
	Vols. 7 and 8 of Bach's *Complete Organ Works* (with Edouard Nies-Berger)
1974	*Was sollen wir tun?* (*A Place for Revelation*, 1988)

Sources for Selections

The quotations in this book were selected from the published works, speeches, sermons, articles, notes, and letters by Albert Schweitzer. Reprinted by kind permission of Mrs. Rhena Schweitzer Miller, the sole heir and keeper of her father's estate.

PUBLICATIONS

The Quest of the Historical Jesus, 1906

The Art of Organ Building and Organ Playing in Germany and France, 1906

J. S. Bach, 1908

The Questionnaire on Organ Construction, 1909

The Mystery of the Kingdom of God, 1914

On the Edge of the Primeval Forest, 1921

Philosophy of Civilization, 1923
Part 1, *The Decay and Restoration of Civilization*
Part 2, *Civilization and Ethics*

Memoirs of Childhood and Youth, 1924

More from the Primeval Forest, 1931

The Mysticism of Paul the Apostle, 1931

Out of My Life and Thought, 1931

Indian Thought and Its Development, 1934

The World of Albert Schweitzer, 1955

The Teaching of Reverence for Life (Collection), 1963

For All That Lives, 1975

SPEECHES &
LECTURES

"My Debt to Goethe," Frankfurt, August 28, 1928

"Religion in Modern Civilization," Oxford, October 16–25, 1934

"Humanity and Peace," Frankfurt, September 16, 1951

"The Problem of Ethics in the Development of Human Thought," Paris, October 20, 1952

"The Problem of Peace in the World of Today," Oslo, November 4, 1954

"A Declaration of Conscience," Oslo, April 23, 1957

"Peace or Atomic War?" Oslo, April 28, 29, 30, 1958

"My Message to Mankind," phonograph record, Lambaréné, 1964

SERMONS

"Creative Suffering," May 14, 1900*

"The Call to Mission," January 6, 1905*

"Overcoming Death," November 17, 1907**

"My Brother's Keeper," April 4, 1909**

"The Peace of God," March 9, 1913*

"The Future of Mankind," October 13, 1918*

"Sacrifice of Others," December 1, 1918*

"Reverence for Life," February 16, 1919*

"Ethics of Compassion," February 23, 1919*

"Conduct Toward Life Around Us: Animals, Plants," March 2, 1919**

"What Does It Mean to Be a Person to Another Person?" June 15, 1919**

   * Published in *Reverence for Life,* 1966

  ** Published in *A Place for Revelation,* 1988

ARTICLES & PAMPHLETS

"The Relations of the White and Colored Races," 1928

"Medical Aid in the Colonies," 1931

"The Revival of Falconry," 1932

"The Round Violin Bow," 1933

"Busy Days in Lambaréné," 1934

"Religion and Modern Civilization," 1934

"Philosophy and the Movement for the Protection of Animals," 1935

"The Ethics of Reverence for Life," 1936

Norman Cousins, 1958, 1959, 1961
Rev. Dr. Timothy Yilsun Rhee, 1958
Serbian Book Association, 1958
Congress of Japanese Physicians, 1959
Youth leader in Germany, 1959
Aida Flemming, 1959
James Sinclair, 1959
Japanese Animal Society, 1961
Rabbi David Jacobson, 1962
President Lyndon B. Johnson, 1962
President John F. Kennedy, 1962, 1963
Jack Anderson, 1963
Elinore Barber, 1963
Queen Juliana of the Netherlands, 1963
Prime Minister Lal Bahadur Shastri, 1964
Rev. Willy Bremi, 1964
Animal Defense League of Canada, 1965
Asiatic Society, 1965
Letter (no name) written shortly before his
     death, 1965
Polish doctor (no name or date)

The Albert Schweitzer Institute for the Humanities

The Albert Schweitzer Institute for the Humanities (ASIH) is a nonprofit, 501(c)(3), nongovernmental organization affiliated with the United Nations. It is dedicated to advancing—through programs of action, research, education, and publication—the philosophy, ideals, and humanitarianism of Dr. Albert Schweitzer in the areas of his own endeavors: medicine and health care, ecology and the environment, philosophy and theology, human rights, animal issues, music and arts, and global order.

The goal of the Albert Schweitzer Institute is to mobilize people and motivate them to action through its seven divisions. Each of these divisions has its own mission statement, goals, and objectives.

1 *Medicine and Health Care Division:* dedicated to providing wider access to health care, and providing humanitarian medical aid, and promoting humanitarian values in the healing arts.

2 *Philosophy and Theology Division:* committed to expanding the understanding and application of Dr. Schweitzer's ethic of Reverence for Life in all of the world's religions and ethical systems.

3 *Ecology and the Environment Division:* organized to promote ethical and realistic solutions to environmental problems and to create an environmentally literate global community composed of individuals who take ecological responsibility for their own actions.

4 *Music and Arts Division:* exists (1) to promote dissemination and discussion of Dr. Schweitzer's musical scholarship and ideas, (2) to foster artistic activity, and (3) to use music education as a means for raising levels of self-confidence, discipline, and creativity.

5 *Animal Issues Division:* dedicated to promoting the ethic of compassion for all living beings through programs that work toward preventing cruelty to animals, alleviating their suffering, and promoting their humane treatment.

6 *Global Order Division:* dedicated to (1) developing programs that promote Reverence for Life as a founding principle of this decade's new global relationships, (2) promoting nonviolent forms of conflict resolution to replace war as a model for the twenty-first century, and (3) working toward rendering obsolete all means of mass destruction.

7 *Human Rights Division:* dedicated to a nonpartisan, pre-emptive international advocacy and education for universal human rights, with a particular emphasis upon the process of the rule of law in protecting human freedom.

Albert Schweitzer's ethic of Reverence for Life and his example, comprehended in the context of today's problems, can serve as a basis for a philosophy of action that can lead to a more peaceful and harmonious world.

The Albert Schweitzer Institute for the Humanities has an unshakable obligation to pass on, from one generation to another, the ideals and example of Albert Schweitzer to inspire humanity, especially youth, to achieve greatness and to serve the common good. Since 1993, ASIH has been affiliated with Quinnipiac College in Hamden, Connecticut, with a branch office in Washington, D.C.

"Reverence for Life comprises the whole ethic of love in its deepest and highest sense. It is the source of constant renewal for the individual and for mankind." It was in this spirit that Albert Schweitzer dedicated his life to humanitarian service; it is in this spirit that the Albert Schweitzer Institute for the Humanities exists today.

For more information, write to:
The Albert Schweitzer Institute
515 Sherman Ave.
Hamden, CT 06514

Index of Sources

Peace on earth.

Albert Schweitzer